THE DUTCH AND THE COROMANDEL COAST

ET RAO N

1

Made with ❤ on the Notion Press Platform
www.notionpress.com

Contents

CHAPTER 1

The Dutch and the Coromandel Coast

From ancient times, the spice trade was one of the essential trades. However, the trade was carried by camel caravans, on land routes, known as Silk Routes. The Silk Road connected Asia with the Mediterranean world, across the Gobi Desert and the Pamir Mountains.

The length of the Silk Road was around 4,000 miles or 6437 Kilometres. Travelling on this route was challenging, as the traders had to confront the intermittent group battles. The group battles were to hold control over the trade and enjoy the benefit from the profits exclusively. The traders continuously used this Road, for more than 1,500 years. The Arab merchants sell the spices for high prices, telling buyers fantastic tales, such as fighting off the winged creatures;

they reach on growing the herb. In the 13th century, spices were distributed to Western and North Europe, from Port Venice. But it was the colossal tariff collecting centre. The European merchants could do little but bear the charges. The distribution business went on till the Ottoman Empire closed off trade with the West.

Now, the European nations, having lost their source of income in spice trade, went on to discover new ways to reach the spice lands. Portugal was the first country that successfully navigated and reached the Spice Islands.

With the development of better navigation equipment, in 1498, Vasco de Gama, the Portuguese traveller sailed across the Indian Ocean with four vessels and reached Calicut, India. This success was a stage for the beginning of the Portuguese spice monopoly in Europe.

Portuguese people are Catholics. They gave the principal distribution of spice business, in North Europe to the Protestants, who formed the majority of the population in the impoverished districts of the Netherlands at that time.

In 1580, crown of Portuguese passed to the King of Spain, who was at war with the protestant people of the Netherlands. So, the Dutch had to forfeit their distribution business. The Dutch after losing their trade tried for direct access to the spice markets, in South Asia.

Jan Huygens van Linschoten was a trader and tourist. In 1563, he was born in Harlem, Holland. He was an executive secretary to the Portuguese Viceroy in Goa, India, from 1583 to 1589. While in employment, he reproduced the top secrets of Portuguese ocean passages to the East-its maps, nautical mile, etc.

After returning to Holland- he printed his work, on sea passages towards the east.

The paper of Jan Huygens's Linschoten fell into the minds of the Dutch.

The work inspired them. They fixed to launch voyages to the east. The dealers and nobles, in Holland, also got motivated by the work of Jan Huygens Van Linschoten and came forward to provide funds for expeditions to spice markets, in South Asia.

At the start, the Dutch shippers and nobles financed individual voyages. Upon the arrival of the fleet, they received their investments. But the expedition involved with compromises and tough at winning, because it comprised of piracy, natural hazard, diseases, and shipwreck, suffering to the merchandise in transport, and dipping of the merchandise value etc.

In 1599, to adjust these losses, they came upon a plan, and that was to unite all twelve-spice sailing Dutch businesses. But the project was not quick, until English East India Company took its birth in Europe.

Now, they formed the United East India Company (Vereenigde Oostindische Compagnie). It was known as the Dutch East India Company.

They built it on March 20, 1602, with funds, from the merged rival Dutch trading companies. They called it a business or a shipping firm and collected additional funds, from the public- by issuing bonds and shares.

Finally, they developed it into the world's, earliest formally listed public company.

The Dutch East India Company (VOC) had the authority to construct territories, wage war, and use soldiers in any other way necessary to increase the company's profits.

VOC established around 22 trading canters/factories, a short distance from each other, on the Coromandel Coast. The factories/trading canters were near the ports, because the ports served as outlets for resources, from the hinterland. The ports were on the ocean or connected with a shallow river. The rivers were perennial but dried up during summer.

The ships of those days were of 300-tonne capacity, and they hardly entered the shallow river.

So, they used flat-bottomed boats for unloading and loading of goods, at sea.

The word Coromandel came from Chola mandalam. It is a region of the Chola Empire of ancient times. Chola is a Tamil word and its meaning is Southern.

During the 17th century, the Coromandel included the coastline of the modern states of Andhra Pradesh and Tamil Nadu with the appendage of the Southern tip of Orissa.

Although Indigo, saltpetre, and cotton yarn were also in the Dutch trade, textiles were the most significant product in Moluccas (Indonesian islands). The Dutch business was only with textiles. In India, they exchanged outside precious metals with textile, and Indian textiles with Indonesian spices. But, Portuguese traded with money.

The VOC trade with Europe was 30%, and it sent the goods, until 1626, straight to the Netherlands. However, after 1626 it despatched goods to Europe, through Batavia (Jakarta, Indonesia).

English entered Coromandel Coast late, and their trading assets, till 1650, compared to VOC, were minimal. In 1622, English trade, from Coromandel Coast was not even 1/6 of the Dutch exports. For a brief period, in 1630, English exports were half of the Dutch exports.

CHAPTER 2

Bhimlipattam(Bheemunipatnam)

The Dutch arrived to Bhimlipattamin 1624. It is 24 KMs. northeast of Visakhapatnam on the Coromandel Coast. It was a commercial canter, for a long time, and a sea-port of Golconda Sultan.

It was prominent, after the Dutch established their factory and Port, here. It was a safe port, for vessel anchoring, in all seasons. The procurement of rice was the chief purpose of the Dutch at Bhimlipattam.

It was an important Dutch settlement on the Coromandel Coast, from 1628 to 1754. They built a fort and factory in 1628.

From the Fort, they purchased local cloth and exported the same to overseas markets, in Batavia (Jakarta, Indonesia). The Fort was under a head (Opperhatd). The head, along with his council, supervised the residents and servants of the Company.

Until 1690, it was under the administration of the Paleacaat (Pulicat) Governor.

Once they arrived, the Dutch fought with the locals. In the fight, 200 locals died. The Dutch also lost 101 soldiers.

Later, the Dutch made peace with the locals and continued their business.

According to Dutch physician, Daniel Hewart, who lived for many years in Paleacaat (Pulicat), called Bhimlipattam- *A rice bowl to Ceylon (Sri Lanka) and other ports.*

The rice, from the river basins was sent from the Kalingapattam (Kalingapattnam) port to Bhimlipattam harbour in coastal boats.

From Bhimlipattam Port, they shipped the rice to Ceylon (Sri Lanka) and other Ports.

By 1663, the Dutch diversified their business into textiles. They purchased cloth, from weavers, at Tuni, Vizagpattam, (Visakhapatnam) Bhimlipattam and sent the delicate material to Batavia (Jakarta, Indonesia) and inexpensive cotton cloth, such as Salempore, to Ceylon (Sri Lanka). The Dutch shipped one thousand bundles of textiles, frequently from the harbor.

The Dutch also exported gingili, gingili oil, hides, skins, seeds, jute, and indigo from this seaport.

From 1665, the Dutch ceased to procure rice, when the Governor of Srikakulam, was aggressively demanding bribe.

It was a resort for a tremendous indigenous shipping fleet. Dutch ships proceeding to Batavia (Jakarta, Indonesia) and Malacca docked at Bhimlipattam to buy rice, meat, and other essentials to meet their onward journey.

After the passing of the Mogul Emperor, Aurangzeb, in 1707, the Administration, in Northern Circars, ruled by Deccan Sultans, collapsed.

The economy was in disorder. The weavers of Bhimli, Tuni, and Vizagpattam, where the export-quality cloth was available, had no jobs. They were short of cash and watching for lenders.

Dutch and French merchants currently had the material at weavers, cost and were searching to export quality clothing. They gave liberal amounts to weavers, under easy payments.

The English merchants paid low salaries to weavers and took the weavers with high-handedness. In contrast to English merchants, the Dutch merchants paid better salaries and allowed extra days for weavers to finish the job. The weavers were eager to sell their clothes to Dutch and French merchants.

In the second decade of the 18th century, villages surrounding Bhimlipattam were burnt, pushing the local vendors to shift.

The Dutch built their trade boats at Bhimlipattam. They raised a lighthouse in 1868, on the Bhimlipattam beach for navigators.

(source: Internet)

In August 1786, a violent incident took place at Bhimlipattam. John Glenn, a German citizen, badly thrashed his housemaid, a thirteen-year-old African teenager, in his residence. The girl did not survive her injuries.

The German was a past English East India Company employee who wed a Dutch Woman. The German served in the Bombay Maritime office, until 1781, before his marriage to the Dutch woman.

The German's finger was cut. He blamed the servant girl for the injury and thrashed her. Unsatisfied with his beating, the German involved a local fisherman-Yellaiah, for an additional fierce beat on her.

Despite the German actions, had his fury out on a teenage girl's body, he was scot-free.

The English East India Company Supreme Judiciary freed him in Calcutta, as he was not their employee.

In Bhimlipattam, the Dutch minted Copper coins with allocations from Vizianagaram Ruler (King). In the local indigenous dialect, dabboo meaning is wealth.

The copper coins were called Copper dub (Copper dabboo), meaning copper money.

(source: Internet)

Figure 1: Dutch cemetery in Bhimli

A Dutch East India Company period (1661-1720) burial ground is at Kummaripaalem in Bhimlipattam town. The grave of Frederick Kessler, who died in 1661, is among the thirteen graves buried here. Those dead between 1762—1945 in Bhimlipattam Port were buried at the Flag Staff Cemetery. The grave of a Dutch infant, William, who died on 5th July 1762, can be found there. Sisters of St. Peter's Church and St. Ann's church (RCM) combined maintain the Flag Staff cemetery.

In Golconda (Hyderabad), after the death of Muzaffar Jung, the Nizam (King), there was fighting, for succession to the throne, in the family.

Charles De Bussy, the general, of the French East India Company, established Salabat Jung as the Nizam, in 1751. In return, in 1753, the crowned, Nizam gave the French General tax collection rights in four northern circars, including Srikakulam, for the support of his troops.

The French- General, Bussy- sent his officer at Masulipattam (Machilipatnam), M. Morcin, to possess his acquisitions.

Jaffar Ali, Faujidar, the tax collector, at Srikakulam, was highly disinclined to give up his charge to the French and opposed Moracin. To strengthen his stand- he called the Marathas from Nagpur, to help him. The Marathas crossed the hills, entered into circars, and devastated it. They fought an irregular action against Moracin. They plundered and burnt the Dutch Bhimli factory (1754) and returned home with immense booty.

After the unfortunate incident, the Bhimli Port lost its prominence, and also the rivalry with the English drove the Dutch from the port. In 1781, the English East India Company occupied the Ports.

[8 9] *Battle of Condore (1758-59): East Godavari district, Andhra Pradesh, India, Zip Code:533 262.*

Santapalli Light House#

It was built by the Dutch in Santapalli village, which is 80 KMs from Visakhapatnam Airport. It is 2 KMs off on the North East to the present Light House. The Light House functioned by burning a log, throughout the night. The object of the Light House was to warn the sailors about the shoal, 6 KMs off the shore. It is now non-functional and in a dilapidated stage.

#Santapalli, Pusapaati Rega Mandal, Vizianagaram district, Andhra Pradesh, India, Pin code:535 204

Golconda[3] (Hyderabad) (1660-1733)

Golconda Fort

In 1660, the Dutch opened a factory in Golconda city. It was an interior factory, but a prime market for Coromandel ports. It attracted foreign merchants to Golconda, owed to the plain and printed varieties of cloth, it produced. In Amsterdam, cotton yarn made in Golconda was in demand.

Golconda was an independent kingdom and -was one of the richest in all India. The domain was extended

---

[1] *Hyderabad, Telangana state, India, Zip Code: 500 008*
[2] *a factory is not a large building, house, or machine but trading station where foreign goods were unloaded and Indian goods were collected, processed, and shipped off.*

to about 480 kilometres in length and 320 kilometres in breadth. It was famous for diamond mines, which induced Aurangzeb, the great Mogul Emperor, to conquer it. There were twenty-three diamond mines in Golconda.

In 1624-25, the Dutch exported 700 tonnes of rice to Indonesia from Golconda, when Java and Batavia (Jakarta) were scarce. This was caused by the making of distilled liquor from rice by the Dutch.

The Golconda[3] Nawab was interested in elephants. After expelling the Portuguese from Ceylon (Sri Lanka), the Dutch started exporting elephants to Golconda. They sold eight elephants to a merchant of Golconda and to the captain of the ship of the Golconda governor.

The Indian Merchants were operating the Dutch Factory with a full staff of ninety members, including ten Dutch officers. Its interpreters, agents, clerks, peons, and carpenters were Indians. The chief merchant was its ambassador. It was enlarged to a complete factory in 1664.

For twenty years, it was a stable market, and the most profitable trading canter of the Dutch East India Company. Later, local unrest caused the trade to diminish, and the Factory was closed in 1733.

CHAPTER 4

Jageranaikapoeram[7]/Jagannadha puram (Kaakinaada) Port (1734-1795)

Coringa[6]: It is a small village, - nearby Hope Island- on the Bay of Bengal- in the East Godavari district of Andhra Pradesh. It is fifteen kilometres southeast of Kaakinaada Port on the Coromandel Coast. Though it is no longer a commercial port in the present century, it was once, a place of great importance.

It was a principal seaport and the only place between Calcutta and Trincomalee-Sri Lanka- where large vessels were docked.

It was an international emporium of trade- in timber- where two to three thousand timber logs were available every year.

It was a bustling Port city. It was also a place for the shipbuilding industry, though only small crafts were built and repaired here. It was because the river at korangi/Coringa- is shallow.

The Dutch had a settlement here, which was closed due to the harassment and extortion of local rulers. It

---

3 A Nawab/Sultan is a Muslim ruler/king

was one place where the best quality of cloth was available.

The port is below sea level; it inundates the land during cyclones and hurricanes.

In December 1789, *a severe* cyclone hit *Korangi/Coringa Port* and took away 20,000 human lives. On 25th November 1834, a second cyclone, which is the world's 3rd worst disaster cyclone, wrecked 20,000 ships, including a French Harmonie vessel sailing- from Libournein France *to Pondicherry (India)* and killed 3, 20,000 people.

The *Port* didn't recover after the second cyclone.

The English shipped their goods from Ingeram, the French from Yaanam (Yaanaon), and the Dutch sent their goods from Jageranaikapoeram /Jagannadhapuram (Kaakinaada). It is south of the Kakinada harbor.

After the disappearance of Coringa Port, from the scene, the Dutch diverted their ships to the Jagannadhapuram-a Kaakinaada suburb. They established their factory there, in 1628. It was a vital textile trading port.

Jageranaikapoeram[7] (Kaakinaada) factory along with Bhimlipattam, in Vizag and Palakollu, in Krishna (districts were under Farmanah, issued by the Nizaam and confirmed by the Mogul Emperor.

They exported tobacco, groundnuts, sugar, and rice from this port.

Chemical fertilizer was their primary import commodity. They were shipping castor oil cakes to Colombo (Sri Lanka) for use in tea and coffee estates. Cheroot was exported to Burma (Myanmaar) from this port. The Dutch were enthusiastic about Jageranaikapoeram (Kaakinaada), though there were several outposts in the neighbouring place. They referred to it as an excellent port, as it was a convenient place to ship goods. The merchants preferred to send their loads to Jageranaikapoeram (Kaakinaada) because it was on the Godavari River inlet and suitable for smooth sailing for ocean-going vessels.

At that time, the average load of ocean–going vessels, was two hundred tonnes.

Labourers from Andhra sailed to Burma (now, Myanmar) through this port. The Dutch controlled the port until 1825.

It was one of the two places the Dutch used to maintain their trade, until the end of the 1825.

---

⁷ East Godavari district, Andhra Pradesh, India, Zip Code: 533 002

The French Officers wounded in the Battle of Condore[8] (1758-59), were in the Jaggeranaikapoeram Fort on parole.

In the 1781 war, the English occupied the Dutch settlements- including Jageranaikapoeram (Kaakinaada), and razed fortified factory houses and buildings.

In 1784, the English returned the factory to the Dutch, as a part of the peace treaty between the contending parties.

During the French Revolution (1785-95) war, the English again took the settlement and returned it in 1818. Finally, in 1825, the English East India Company took over the Port.

Tuni[9]: It was a centre for weaver villages. It is on the Coromandel Road, from Masulipattam (Machilipatnam) to Vizagapatam (Viskhapatnam). It is eighty kilometers south of Visakhapatnam.

Dutch and English traders were attracted to this place- for the coarse and delicate variety of cloth produced here.

Peddapuram[10]: It is near *Jaggeranaikapoeram/* Jagannadhapuram and close to Coringa port.

The cloth produced, in the village was supplied in

[9] *East Godavari district, Andhra Pradesh, India, Zip code: 533 437*

large quantities to the Dutch. It was a suitable place for washing and bleaching large amounts of fabric.

Around two hundred-washer man families were working here during those days. They depended on the local textile industry for their livelihood.

Yaanaon[11] **(Yaanam)**: Yaanaon was once the Dutch colony, before the French occupied it, in 1723. It is 9 kilometres distant from the Bay of Bengal- on the Coromandel Coast. It is on the bank of the Godavari delta, at the confluence of Godavari River and its tributary Coringa.

The town is a mixture of Telugu and French customs. The Dutch built a fort here- under the name- Saalikota. Later, weavers occupied the fort. It is one of the signs- showing the presence of the Dutch at Yaanaon.

The Dutch minted coins at Neelapalli, a village 3 kilometres from Yaanaon (Yaanaam), and protected them in the Saalikota Fort. The Dutch traded in cotton, silk, opium, and rice.

Recently, in the west of Yaanaon (Yaanaam), while digging the earth, some wells were unearthed. They were the containers, of the Dutch period. In these containers the Dutch were mixing indigo. They were known as indigo wells (Neelikundaloo).

---

[10]*East Godavari district, Andhra Pradesh, India, Zip Code: 533 401*

CHAPTER 5

Daatzeram[12]/ (Draakshaaraamam) (1633-1730)

In 1633, the Dutch established a factory at Daatzeram (Draakshaaraamam). It consisted of 24 local laborers working under four Dutch supervisors. Washer men from nearby Gollapalem[13] and Gokavaram[14] villages worked exclusively- for the Dutch.

There were, as many as, fifteen villages, around this place, where weaving was the main profession. Since 1617, the Dutch had bought guinea cotton cloth, from this place. Evidence dated July 21, 1617 reported- a Dutch company servant, Hendrick De Witt, was assisting the Dutch- in buying the textiles from this place. It was a vital marketing centre.

They exported leather to Batavia (Indonesia) and Japan- through Masulipattam (Machilipatnam) port.

A piece of evidence- dated 28th November 1623 revealed there was a shortage of funds, at Palakol (Paalcollu) and Daatzeram (Draakashaaraamam). In addition, new Havaldar at Masulipattam (Machilipatnam)

---

[12] *East Godavari district, Andhra Pradesh, India, Zip code: 533 202;*
[13] *East Godavari district, Andhra Pradesh, India, Zip Code: 533 468;*
[14] *East Godavari district, Andhra Pradesh, India, Zip Code: 533 286*

port was placing, many hindrances, on the Dutch East India Company's trade. Whatever was the reason, the Dutch closed the factory in 1654.

In 1659, however they returned to the Daatzeram (Draakshaaraamam) market again, to prevent the English East India Company from entering this place.

At Vollendu Dibba (Hollander's mound) there are two sculpturally covered Dutch tombs of the (1675-1728) periods.

The word Vollendu refers to the local pronunciation of Hollanders' and the local meaning for Dibba is a mound.

Injaram[15]**:** In 1708, the Dutch established their trade settlement- in Injaram. It is near Yaanaon. The weavers of this place worked exclusively for the Dutch.

In the words of **English East India Company's *Captain Hamilton***, the cloth weaved at Injaram was "The best and most exceptional quality of fabric in India".

The local rulers' greediness and extortion of money from the exported cloth by Golconda officials- ruined the Dutch trade at Injaram.

---

[15]*Taallaraevu - Mandal, East Godavari- district, Andhra Pradesh, India, Pin Code: 533 464*

CHAPTER 6

Nagulavancha[16] (1669-1687)

Nagelwanza was a famous centre of indigo[17] and mango orchids. Indigo is used in dyeing handloom fabrics, and Nagelwanza (Naagulavancha) indigo was considered the best.

European markets sought indigo-dyed handloom fabrics. The Dutch, tempted by the demand for handloom fabrics, searched for the topography of Nagelwanze /(Naagulavancha).

Nagelwanze /(Naagulavancha) was a large village with three smaller towns, and four market streets.

There were 200 textile merchants, 150 weavers, 100 cultivators, 20 copper workers, 15 ironsmiths, 20 goldsmiths, 20 dyers and 150 Brahmin houses in the village. There were 20 accountants, 15 bullock cart drivers, and many metalworkers in these houses.

Ten temples were in the village; five worshipped Lord Shiva, and the remaining five were dedicated to Lord Vishnu.

---

[16] *Khammam district, Telangana State, India, Zip Code: 507 208;*
[17] *Indigo is a blue powder, obtained from the plants of the genus Indi gofers, and they used as a dye.*

The Nagelwanze /(Naagulavancha) village had twenty mango tree plantations, and ten tanks.

In 1669, the Dutch established their camp at Nagelwanze / (Nagulavancha) to monitor the quality of goods made there. In 1670, they began construction of the factory, and appointed Havartis, as the first chief of the factory. In the same year, they constructed a building, in the middle of the village, to house the first and second chiefs of the factory. The building was called a lodge.

The Dutch were the first to set up the factory.

It was one of the earliest interior trading-and fabric export centres of the Dutch East India Company. French did not visit this place.

The Dutch had two horses, two stables, and two gardens in Nagelwanze / (Naagulavancha). One Park was outside the village, and the other was beyond the stable.

In 1678, they sold the horses. In the empty stables, they carried dying and nailed forging work. The Dutch wanted to increase production, considering the higher demand for Nagelwanze / (Naagulavancha) fabric- in the European markets.

The Dutch not only ruled, but also, harassed the villagers. They turned the business camp into a political power base. Consequently, the villagers revolted against the Dutch.

On 13-10-1687 the villagers raided the lodge, killed the merchants, the first and second chief of the Factory, and buried them in the garden outside the village.

Besides textiles, the Dutch exported essential items like clay, mud, cotton, emery stone, and saltpetre, iron, and indigo.

They were also exporting handloom products and mangoes.

The below given Dutch East India Company officers served in the Nagelwanze/Naagulvancha:
The First Chief: Nicolaas Faber (1668-75) (Founder of the company & First superior) - (Born on 05-04-1628 at Amsterdam & Died on 08-02-1675)
Merchant: Abraham Vander Voort(1668-76)- (Born in Zeeland)- (Born on 04-10-1640 & Died on 06-05-1676)
The Second Chief: Jacob Corbusier (1676-1679)
The Second Chief: Abraham Vander-Voort (1676-76)
The Second Chief: Dirk Vonk(1676-78)
The Second Chief: Nicolas Bolk (1678-79)

The First Chief: Ambrosius Vander weil (1679-84)
The Second Chief: Barent Houthhuyn(1679-82)

The Second Chief: Nicolaas Dankwaard (1682-84)
The First Chief: Adrian Block (1684-86)
The Second Chief: Nicolaas Dankwaard (1684-86)
The First Chief: Nicolaas Dankwaard (1686-87)
The Second Chief: Gerard Benoorden (1686-87)

CHAPTER 7

PALIKOL[18] (Paalakollu)
(1613-1781) (1785-1795) (1818-1825)

The Dutch had settled in Palikol (Paalakollu)- when Charles II was King in England.

Palikol was a village in the Godavari district, 8 kilometers north of Narsapur (Narsaapuram), on the canal from Vijjeswaram to Narsapur (Narsaapuram).

The Dutch noticed that a large part of the textiles they were exporting from Masulipattam (now, Machilipatnam) Port was coming from Palikol (now, Paalakollu). So, they decided to erect a factory at Palikol.

In 1613, they obtained a Farmanah from the ruler of Palikol, Quli Qutub Shah of Golconda

The sultan/ruler leased- to the Dutch, for an annual payment of 1000 pagodas.

In 1658, the Factory functioned with 700 labourers, under 8-10 Dutch national's supervision. They were engaged in weaving, dyeing, bleaching, and washing.

In addition to textiles, the Dutch exported leather, to

---

[18] *West Godavari district, Andhra Pradesh, India, Pin code: 534 260*

other countries from Palikol, via Masulipattam (Machilipatnam). They also exported lamp oil, wood, leopard and rhinoceros' skin, bricks, and roof tiles from Palikol.

The Dutch had a small residential building and a storehouse for textiles. It had facilities for washing finished goods.

The soil around the village was very fertile. The Dutch took advantage of it and grew- oranges and plantains.

In 1676 an excellent rice-producing, the neighbouring village, Conteru [19], (Konteru), was added.

The Dutch also established several works for making ropes, cords, yarn, and thread from hump for sail-cloth ships.

On October 4, 1679, the English East India Company Agent (of the coast and Bay) at Fort St. George, Fernandez Navarrete Streynsham,came to Narsapur (Narsaapur) for inspection.

The Dutch chief at Palikol stayed at the Dutch house in Narsapur, on that day to call on the Agent, as a courtesy.

---

[19] *West Godavari district, Andhra Pradesh, Pincode: 534 260*

The Dutch abandoned the factory in 1730.

Under the Treaty of Paris, in 1783, they ceded, Palikol to the British, but they continued to pay rent- until 1804.

The English restored it to Dutch in 1818.

The Dutch finally surrendered Palikol to the English in 1824.

There were several graves, of that period, of which two graves still exist, and belong to the Chief of Factor & Merchant, Simon Van Grooenewegen of Delft-(who died on 03-6-1665) and Lambert Hensinck- (born in Palikol and died on 09-11-1662).

CHAPTER 8

Narsapur[20] (Narsaapuram) (1618-1825)

The Dutch found the Port, in 1173. *From 1570-1700 Narsapur (Narsaapuram) was a synergetic shipbuilding centre in South India.*

The Dutch landed there in 1626. It was the centre for manufacturing long cloth. The chintz manufactured at Masulipattam (Machilipatnam) was from this long cloth.

A few villages surrounding Narsapur (Narsaapuram) were famous for cotton goods. Here, weavers and painters were readily available. The weavers produced coarsely woven cotton cloth and a few quantities of painted fabric.

High-quality timber was abundantly available here. J. Ovington, an English chaplain, who visited India in 1690, said that the Indian teak was firmer than the English oak. He urged the English to use the Indian timber as it helped them in the war due to being strong enough, that it would not crack even by the force of a bullet. The skill of Indians in shipbuilding impressed him-and He said that Indians even outshone Europeans.

---

[20]*West Godavari district, Andhra Pradesh, India, Zip/ Pin code: 534 275*

Modapollem/ (Mahadevayyapaalem), an adjoining town, was known for timber and cotton. Shipbuilding materials like rope, coir, and nails were produced. Skilled and cheap labourers were locally available there.

Narsapur (Narasaapuram) iron workers were highly skilled- at those times, and in Narsapur, nearly 40,000/- pounds worth of nails was annually made.

In 1661, Golconda's ruler, Abdul Hassan Taanishaa, granted a piece of land in Narsapur (Narasaapuram) for the Dutch to build houses. The Dutch used the ground, for a carpentry workshop and ironsmith.

On 16th April, 1679, English East India Company, Fort St. George, Agent (the later, the designation was Governor) visited the trading centre and found around 300 ironsmiths were carrying forge. Also, many boats were engaged in the Narsapur seaport to load rice to Gingee/Jinji[21] Fort. He observed that spotted deer was available in Narsapur (Narasaapuram), and they were bred by the Dutch agents and factors

The Dutch exported cotton and teak wood from this place.

---

[21]*Gingee is the English form of the Tamil word Sinj. Later the English and French called it Ginjee or Jinji. The early records give the spelling as Chinjee or Chengey. It is in Villipuram district, Tamil Nadu, India, Zip Code: 605 402.*

In the early 17th century, Narsapur emerged as a convention yard for shipbuilding and repair. Dutch trading vessels were built at Narsapur.

The English East India Company damaged ship 'The Advice' was sent to Narsapur for repair, in October 1641.

The ships built here were for the Golconda Sultan to despatch rice for distribution, as alms in Mecca, and for traveling of Hajj pilgrims to Mecca. At Narsapur **Thomas Bowrey[22]** - referred that a 1,000-ton ship was built for the Golconda Sultan (King) fleet- for sailing in the Bay of Bengal and the Arabian Sea

Besides Dutch and English, other merchant ships were also built here. The artisans produced 600 tonnes and above-capacity boats with excellent timber and iron.

Vessels up to 300 tonnes could only enter the Godavari River at Narsapur. Hence, goods, from Paalicol and Narsapur were carried 80 kilometers south of Narsapur, in flat-bottomed boats, for loading them into large vessels, at Masulipattam (Machilipatnam).

For over two centuries, Narsapur was accredited for docks and the repair of vessels. It was a Metro politian

---

[22]Thomas Bowery (1659-1713) was an English merchant and mariner.

port of the eighteenth century.

English authorities were unhappy with the Indian enterprise entering shipbuilding. So, on 2nd February, 1622, King Charles II of England ordered that no Englishman should pass on knowledge of shipbuilding to those outside England. Further, he called strict punishment for violators.

The storms and floods destroyed Narsapur town and drowned many people and cattle.

A cyclone, in 1666, hit Narsapur (Narasaapuram) and beat the Dutch dockyard. Under its impact, a new under-commission ship was buried under 7 feet of-sand, and another boat went underneath the 4.5 feet of sand.

Vaalendu (Hollander's) raevu, in Narsapur (Narasaapuram), was once Hollander's bathing place.

CHAPTER 9

Masulipattam[23] (Machilipattam) (1605-1756)

Masulipattam Port in the 17th century

Masulipattam (Machilipatnam) was a poor fishing town, which gave it, its name.

During the first century, after Christ, the town was noted for the manufacturing of muslin.

The port was known to the Egyptian merchants, as Masula. It was also known as Bandar-I-Mubarak, in the

---

23 *Krishna district, Andhra Pradesh, India, Pin Code: 521 001*

Indo-Persia-Chronicles of the late Qutub Shahi period.

It was the Chief Maritime Port and hub of international diamond trade during Golconda's reign. Its custom was per annum 14,000 pagodas. It was, once the most important and, fourth largest city in India, after Delhi, Ahmadabad and Surratt. In 1673, the number of inhabitants was approximately 200,000.

The town was famous for the most beautiful calicoes, with different colours and artistic works. In the 16th century, though they did not possess a factory, the Portuguese were also trading on cloth.

The Dutch were the first Europeans to establish a factory on the Coromandel Coast at Masulipattam (Machilipatnam). In 1603, under Admiral Steven Van der Hagen, a fifteen-vessel fleet left the Netherlands for Aachen.

Out of the fifteen boats, one boat, Yacht Delft, under Paulus Van Soldt, in February 1605, sailed from Aachen and landed at Masulipattam (Machilipatnam).

With the help of a Jewish resident of the Golconda, Soldt secured the, right for trade at Masulipattam (Machilipatnam).

Pieter Ysaacx was appointed as the first chief of the trading centre, and several employees were hired, to work under him.

Golconda Sultan Quli Kutub Shah (1518-1611) rented out the Masulipattam (Machilipatnam) Port for eight lakhs, it was, in turn, rented to sub-bidders. The sultan exempted them from payment of a 2.5% disembarkment fee.

The sub-bidders were exploiting the traders. The Dutch, irked with the exploitation of bidders, led a delegation under Paulus Van Soldt and Willensz Augusttam to complain to the Golconda Sultan,Mohammed Quli Qutub Shah.

The Golconda Sultan allowed the Dutch to pay 4% duty on export and import. Also, the Sultan exempted the weavers, dyers, bleachers, and other artisans from paying 12% stamp duty on linen cloth. Further, he allowed, their direct access to the Dutch. This privilege-was given only to the Dutch, among the Europeans.

Though, the Dutch trade centre was established, in 1605, their active trade began, in 1669-three years after the English settlement.

Peter Ayliff and Willensz Augusttam were the first in charge of Dutch trade at Masulipattam (Machilipatnam) port. As of 26-3-1679, Signor Outhorne was the Dutch chief at Masulipattam (Machilpatnam) Port.

Five varieties of cloth were available in Masulipattam (Machilipatnam) area. The guineas variety, known as plain cloth or bafta, was exported to Batavia (Jakarta, in Indonesia) and West Africa, for enslaved people.

The rich and noble families in Holland were wearing salampore cloth and they liked it. To meet the demand for it, Gerrit Van Westrenen (1692-1743), the head merchant at Masulipattam ordered large quantities of the cloth, and exported them from Masulipattam. It had earned good profit to the VOC.

By 1682, the Dutch exported 48, 44,500 yards of the cloth from Masulipattam Port. Muslin, Zaree was also shipped from the Port. Fancy goods and diamonds were other exports of Dutch from this Port.

Indigo produced in Nagelwancha[16] (Naagulavancha) was regularly shipped to Holland from Masulipattam (Machilipatna) Port.

After 1606, the Dutch couldn't compete commercially with the Portuguese, in the commodity-trade, at Masulipattam (Machilipatnam). They diverted to the- profitable-slave trade. The export of enslaved people to Batavia (Jakarta, Indonesia) and Java was more essential to them than- other-exports. They captured enslaved people from the Golconda kingdom.

From 1622 to 1630, they shipped 2,275 enslaved people. The enslaved people were sent to work in the Dutch plantations and factories.

In 1629, the Dutch exported 96,000 pounds of Iron and 20,000 pieces of steel to Jakarta.

The Dutch were trading in elephants too. An elephant purchased for 200 Spanish Reales at Kedah in (Malaya) was sold in Masulipattam (Machilipatnam) for fifteen times the cost.

The Deccan Sultan issued licenses to the Dutch and other Europeans to mint rupee and other denomination coins with their emblem. The duty of minting was shared between the Sultan and the Dutch.

After the conquest of Golconda by the Mughals in 1687, the trade was destroyed. The Masulipattam (Machilipatnam)- Golconda (Hyderabad) highway became unsafe, due to bandits.

Masulipattam (Machilipatnam), port is one of the cyclone-prone areas in the Bay of Bengal. Under Vaalendu Paalem (Hollanders' locality) Golconda Sultan gave land to the Dutch, to construct residential houses.

Some Dutch settled here and lived with their families, after being discharged, from company service.

In 1660 and 1662, severe storms hit the Masulipattam (Machilipatnam) coast- and the flood washed away- a large portion of the town. In 1662 another storm- devoured thirty vessels and drowned many people.

The Vaalendu (Holland) Paalem locality, within Masulipattam (Machilipatnam), is at an elevated area. In an April 1679 cyclone, the winds swept away buildings and, the bridge that- linked the port and town- were submerged underwater. The Dutch gave shelter to the flood-affected people.

Another cyclone on 1st November in 1864 hit the city of Masulipattam (Machilipatnam). A tidal wave 13ft high went 27 kilometres in- land and destroyed everything in its path.

Thirty thousand residents were killed and the Port was damaged.

CHAPTER 10

DIVI SEEMA[24] or Deevi (Island) (1669-1687)

Deevi (Island), is a combination of two words. Deevi- means Island, in the local language and Seema means a region or area. So, it is an island region- 35 kilometres from Masulipattam (Machilipatnam) port, and 65 kilometres from Vijayawada. It is at the mouth of one of the branches of Krishna River and surrounded by shoals- for six miles south and east. Deevi Island has been cut off from the mainland, throughout the year, by the creeks of the river Krishna. It is unsuitable for a harbour, but the Dutch wanted to deepen the channel and develop the island, for navigation and shift their trade from Masulipattam (Machilipatnam) port to Deevi Island. They tried for the island, with their rulers, but were unsuccessful.

The region rich in Chaaya root[25], made the region rich in chintz production. When the English trade in Masulipattam (Machilipatnam) declined, in 1699, the English embassy, led by Sir William Norris, went to the Mogul Emperor, Aurangzeb, and requested him to cede the Deevi-island to English.

The emperor did not consider the request.

---

[24] Krishna district, Andhra Pradesh, India, Zip code: 521 132
[25] A plant used for making an excellent dye.

44

CHAPTER 11

Petapoeli[26] (Peddapally) (now, Nizampatnam) (1606-1668)

The Dutch occupied the city, from 1606 to 1668, for trading. Natively known as Peddapally, it was referred to as Petapoeli, by the Dutch.

The English called it Pettipoly- a beautiful village with two- kilometre-long seashore. It had commercial relations with other countries, before Christ.

Pliny[27] and Ptolemy[28] mentioned Motupalli -a suburban port of Petapoeli- in their writings. It is an obscure fishing village now, but it was a famous seaport during Kaakatiya's reign.

Marco Polo, a Venetian traveller, visited the port around 1287, referring to Motupalli as Mutfill in his travelogue, and extensively describing the reigning Kaakateeya queen, Rudrama Devi.

Before to the Dutch, the town was controlled by the Portuguese- between 1505 and 1640 and was under the reign of Golconda Sultan.

---

[26] *Petapoeli (Peddapally), Guntur district, Andhra Pradesh, India, Zip Code: 522 314*
[27] *Pliny the elder- and Italian was commander of the fleet in the Bay of Naples and author of 'Natural History.*
[28] *Ptolemy-ancient Greek mathematician, astronomer, geographer and music theorist.*

In 1606, Paulus Van Soldt made a second voyage to Coromandel Coast from Bantam (Jakarta, Indonesia). He anchored in Petapoeli and established a trading post. It was the second most important port after Masulipattam. Petapoeli was independent and equal in status to Masulipattam. In August 1606, Mir Jumla, Mughal army chief at Golconda, helped the Dutch get Farmanah[8] from the Golconda Sultan at Petapoeli.

The Sultan fixed the export toll at 4% and import toll at 4%, on the Dutch merchandise, throughout the kingdom of Golconda. The Dutch were also exempted from stamp duty on cloth and 12% track duty, which was exempted to local traders only.

Petapoeli (Peddapally) is surrounded by weaving villages. They shipped enormous lengths of long clothes, murries, Salempur, lungees, painted calicoes of diverse sorts, saltpetres, iron and steel overseas.

The Dutch used to send goods in light boats north and south from its neighboring ports, Motupalli, Kothapatnam, and Ramappapura.

The territory is famous for the finest dye root, second in quality to Pulicaat[29]; hence they delivered the finest quality of colored and dyed goods to the world, from here. The land was suitable for giving the finest dye root. It was second in quality to Pulicat. An island near the port, was giving the best quality dye root.

After establishing an English trading post at Petapoeli (Peddapally), the Dutch competed with the English for saltpeter.

The Dutch imported at Petapoeli - woolens, woolens, pearls, iron, copper, glass wares, polished beads and boxes of money.

They imported long pepper at Paliacatta (Pulicat)[29]. It was abundant and cheap in Sumatra.

Petapoeli was a center for shipbuilding and it had the largest harbor on the Coromandel Coast. During the 17th century, higher tonnage ships regularly docked at the seaport. The English East India Company Agent at Fort St. George, Streynsham Master, said in 1677 - "Sea-going vessels of 50 to 100 tonnes were visiting the port".

Until 1609, Petapoeli was an autonomous port, and equal in status to Masulipattam Port. Both had separate governors and were endowed with- exclusive rights in making business decisions. But the Masulipattam governor and the Petapoeli governor contacted each other over every business deal- that was a complicated issue with natives.

But, in 1609, the Dutch at their meeting in Bantam, resolved to do away with individual governors for Masulipattam and Petapoeli and replace with a general governor for Masulipattam and Petapoeli. Then Petapoeli came under the governor of Masulipattam.

In the beginning, the conditions in Petapoeli were less uncongenial than in Masulipattam.

From 1609, the Havildar at Petapoeli emulated his associate at Masulipattam and harassed the Dutch.

Van Wick went to Golconda to complain against Havildar at Petapoeli, and about his money extortion. But he returned to Petapoeli, in January 1610, without solving the issue.

The relations that existed between the Dutch and Golconda Sultan changed, after the English moved to Petapoeli (Peddapally). It sank from social, to severe.

Petapoeli (Peddapally) was the Port name, until 1679, and since then, its name, has been Nizampattnam Port.

CHAPTER 12

PALIACATTA[29] (now, PULICAAT) (1610-1781) (1785-1795) (1805-1825)

It was the capital, and headquarters of the Dutch East India Company, on the Coromandel Coast. It is 60 kilometres from Chennai.

It was centrally situated, to trade, both in the north and south. Weavers' villages surrounded the port, and ten thousand handlooms were operated. Handloom goods were exported from this port.

There was a dangerous reef off the shore, so more substantial ships were avoiding the port. Also, the river flowing into the sea allowed vessels of less than 50 tonnes.

On 26th April, 1606, the Dutch under Van Soldt made a second voyage to Coromandel Coast from Batavia (Jakarta, Indonesia), in the vessel Delft. They stopped on the shores of Karimanal village near Paliacatta (Pulicaat), to negotiate trade with local merchants- in the town.

The negotiations did not succeed, due to the conspiracy of the Portuguese with the locals.

---

[29] *Ponneri, Tiruvallur district, Tamil Naadu, Zip Code : 601 205*

In 1609, to escape the tyranny and oppression of Golconda officials at Masulipattam (now, Machilipatnam) and Petapoeli (Peddapalli), the Dutch drove towards the south. It landed near the shores of Paliacatta (Pulicaat), for fresh water.

The Arab merchants near the shore helped them with food and water.

An understanding of trade materialized between the Dutch and Arab merchants. They traded textiles, in exchange for spices. In April 1610, the Dutch opened a trade centre at Paliacatta (Pulicaat) and appointed Hans Marcelis as the chief factor. To assist him, four employees were recruited.

On one unfortunate day, Shahbandar's[30] men instigated by the Portuguese, thrashed Hans Mercelis. They looted the factory and his men. But fortunately, the local King Venkatapathy Raju or King Venkata II came to their help and permitted to the Dutch to build a factory. He turned against Portuguese, and ordered them to leave the territory.

The Dutch built the factory, on the foundations of a Portuguese factory and appointed a director. It was the first and highest appointment (Director) of the Dutch on the Coromandel Coast.

---

[30] *Shahabunder: Officer in charge of the Port.*

In 1612, the Portuguese sacked Weimar Van Berchem, one of the directors of their company. Weimar joined the Dutch East India Company, at Paliacatta (Pulicat).

In October 1612, he-led Dutch missions to the Vijayanagar ruler court in Vellore and got a new cowl[31] on 12th December, 1612.

According to the new cowl, the toll was fixed at 1% for imports and 2% for exports, and a neighbouring village, Venadu, was granted to the Dutch territory.

Thus, the advancements of Dutch reduced the prospects of the Portuguese, in the territory.

The significant trading of the Dutch at that time was textiles and diamonds.

In Europe, the long cloth of Paliacatta (Pulicaat) was very famous. The King and Queen of the Netherlands-were wearing Paliacatta(Pulicaat) chemise. The cotton fabrics, available along the Coromandel Coast were in demand, in Ormuz, Aden, Arabia, and Africa.

The printed cloth of Paliacatta (Pulicaat) was exported to Achen, Bantam, Malaysia, Singapore, and European countries.

---

[31] *An agreement for lease.*
Havaldar: A top post in the kingdom has particular importance, and his office is a stepping-stone to a higher placement in the government.

The Coromandel cloth was exchanged for Persian horses, seed pearls, sulphur, and dry fruits. The Paliacatta (Pulicaat) merchants bartered Indian colour cotton stuff for Burma rubies. Regularly 4-5 ships with textiles left for Pegu from Paliacatta(Pulicaat) to fetch gold and rubies. From the 16th century Paliacatt (Pulicaat) had regular trade with Pegu. Raw precious stones were sent from Pegu, for polishing by expert artisans in Paliacatta (Pulicat).

The Dutch shipped pepper, pearls, and other items in bulk to their settlements and exported Diamonds to Europe.

Paliacatta (Pulicat) was also considered to supply the best chayaroot.

Large quantities of silver from Laos were sent to Pulicat. Lac was also imported, at Paliacatta (Pulicat).

In 1613, with the help of Queen Irabu-the wife of King Venkata II, the Dutch used a Portuguese foundation to build a fort, called castle Geldria, near the shores of Paliacatta (Pulicat) lake.

The fort was 7 meters high and 535 meters in circumference.

They christened it Fort Geldria, after Gelderland (a state in Netherlands) the native place of the Director of Coromandel coast and factories.

In 1617, it was the seat of the Dutch chief and headquarters of the Dutch administration. By 1619, the Dutch chief, -at the Fort Geldria, was promoted and accorded the title of Governor, and the extraordinary Counsellor of the Dutch East India Company.

Before 1617, the Dutch Coromandel was under the Dutch Ceylon Government.

In July 1613, within one month of its completion, the fort was attacked by a local chieftain- Ethiraj, who was with the Portuguese. After he was suppressed, the Portuguese attacked the fort, from both land and sea. They were also thrown out.

In 1618, the fort was fortified by Gouden Leeuwin with 130 Dutch soldiers and 32 guns. It was a center of defense. Many refugees took shelter in it, during local disturbances- in the kingdom.

In 1621, the Dutch allowed the English, to have a settlement at Paliacatta (Pulicat).

The Portuguese again attacked the Dutch, in 1623 and burnt two ships- at the harbour.

In August, 1624 the Company entered into an understanding with local chieftains to spare Pulicat from future attacks.

By December 1629, the situation in Paliacatta (Pulicat) was under control, but the company had trouble in South Coromandel Coast.

In 1632, the Vijayanagar ruler Raama Deva Raayalu died, and there was a civil war in the kingdom, and cotton-producing villages were burnt.

An attack on Pulicat by chieftain, Timmaraju- was prevented by the timely offering of money by the Dutch.

In 1633, the Portuguese, expecting land support from the Vijayanagar ruler, attacked the Dutch But, the Vijayanagar ruler (King) did not keep his promise and the Portuguese attack failed.

After the Portuguese withdrew from the scene, the Vijayanagar ruler, King Sri Ranga III, residing at Chandragiri attacked the Dutch at Paliacatta (Pulicaat) and collected a handsome tribute.

By 1689, the Head Quarters of the Dutch East India Company at Paliacatta (Pulicaat) and Ceylon (Sri Lanka) moved to Nagapattam (Nagapattinam)43.

With the Headquarter shifting, the Fort was reduced to 18 guns, and 40 men and it had not recovered, until 1714.

In 1781, the Dutch moved their headquarters back to Fort Geldria, after the English seized Nagapattinam.

The English East India Company sent Major Elphinston, from Madras, with orders to destroy the Fort after capture.

On 3rd July, 1781, the Dutch surrendered the Fort to the English.

The dyeing of textiles and trading of fabrics went on to flourish. The change of power could not affect the success of the Fort-as a trading post.

The Dutch surrendered the fort to the English East India Company in 1795. Before transferring ownership, the Dutch blew up the defence.

As per the Anglo-Dutch Treaty of, 1824, the Dutch had to abandon all the properties and establishments to the English by 1825.

Accordingly, Dutch resident Obdam, ceremoniously transferred, the trade centre to English East India Company man, Crawley, on 01-06-1825.

Palicatta (Pulicaat) was the capital of the Dutch for two terms from (1610-1690) and (1781-1825).

Figure 4: Fort-Geldria

Now, the Dutch Fort, Geldria is in ruins. The local traders occupied the Dutch houses. A 1640- constructed building, which the Dutch Governor used for tax collection, is dilapidated. Paliacatta(Pulicaat) was the capital and headquarters of Dutch East India Company from 1610 to 1690 and from 1781 to 1825. During this period, the following were a few Governors who held the office:

Peter Isaac Eloff(1608-1610
Carel Reyniersz(1636-1638)
Cornelis Speelman(1663-1665)
Henry Francis von So lister(1824-1825)

Slave trade: The Dutch could not commercially compete with the Portuguese. Hence, they- diverted toward the slave trade. The demand for labourers in

Dutch colonies made this a beneficial arrangement. The slave trade benefited them, as there was a demand for labourers in Dutch colonies.

The Dutch were procuring slaves through brokers- at Chennai and from there; the slaves were shipped to Dutch settlements.

According to Richard and B Allen's book," The European Slave trade, in the Indian Ocean"- between 1624 and 1665, eleven thousand slaves- from the Arakan province, in Myanmar were shipped to Dutch colonies.

For the 1645 revolt, 2118 slaves were shipped to Batavia (now Jakarta, Indonesia)

Also, enslaved people were brought to Paliacatta (Pulicaat) from Dutch settlements-Tegenapattinam, Karriakkal, and Bengal. There they were sold in Dutch currency, from 4 to 40 Guilders. The slave rate was not uniform. It fluctuated from year to year- dropping during famines, battles or revolts against rulers.

The Dutch continued the slave trade, till 1700. Again in late 1700, the Dutch shipped slaves to Mauritius from Bhimlipattam (Bheemunipatnam), Jaggernaikpoeram/Jagannathapurm7 and Paliacatta(Pulicaat)[29]

Mint: In 1615, Dutch Government's mint and gunpowder factory were established. Dutch minted gold Pagoda coins at Paliacatta (Pulicaat). They stamped the image of the Hindu God, Lord Venkateswara, on the coins. In 1657 MirJumla, the Golconda army chief, permitted the Dutch to mint rupee coins in Paliacatta (Pulicaat) mint. In 1726 the Dutch issued copper coins, in their territories, on the Coromandel Coast.

The Paliacatta (Pulicaat) minted coins had a high reputation. They yielded a profit of 3.5 %, on their trade at Masulipattam (now,Machilipatnam), and- a mint duty at the rate of 5.5 %, at the mint.

Tombs: In Paliacatta (Pulicaat) a cemetery with 76 graves, carved in Dutch architectural style, is preserved.

(source:Internet)

Figure 5: Dutch cemetery in Pulicat

Some of the cemeteries in Pulicat:

1. Peter Matheson - Captain of East India Company- died on 9th February 1658 (at the age of 51 years)
2. Jaques Cuillier - (Born in Ghent in 1620) Governor and Director of Coromandel Coast
3. Died on 5th November, 1679(at the of 59 years)
4. Lady Joanna Berio-widow of diseased Abraham Floris Zoon Bolwerk- died on 18th May 1684(at the age of 70 Years)
5. Heer Willem Van Dielen- (Born in Haarlem) Over merchant, second over @ Chief of Masulipattam (now, Machilipatnam) died on 13th October 1688.
6. Dirk Both (Born in Utrecht, Netherlands)- a merchant & third chief in the castle of Geldria. died on 24th June, 1719 (at the age of 31 years)

CHAPTER 13
Armugaon[32]

It is a small port 56 kilometers north of Paliacatta (Pulicaat) and 24 kilometers south of Krishnapatnam Port. It is on the left bank of the river Upputaeru. It offered excellent anchorage facilities because of the shoal. The Dutch established their Factory in 1628 to get rid of money-extracting officials at Masulipattam and Petapoeli(Peddapally).

It is one of the earliest factories on the East Coast of India. The river and port provided excellent anchorage facilities to European vessels. The land belonged to Venkatagiri Rajah. It is sometimes- called Durgaraazapattinam or Duggaraazaapatnam after a neighbouring village, seven miles north of Armugaon on the Buckingham canal, where open communication with the sea can be maintained.

In a neighbouring village, called Monapalem, a circular mason lighthouse worked from 1853. It is the only lighthouse near Armugaon, that warns vessels of the -shoal that is around 9.6 kilometers from shore 16 kilolmetrers long. Durgaraazapattinam (Duggaraazaapatnam) is also called Blackwood's Harbour after a naval officer, Sir Henry Black Wood, who found the place, before other Europeans and suggested that it would make a practical harbour.

Patnaswaamula Armogam Mudaliar was a local village accountant, known as "Karanam". Rajah Venkatagiri from gave him the site for the construction

---

of a factory. Patnaswaamula Armogam Mudaliar developed it into a Port. After his name, the port is called Armugaon.

He permitted the traders, on the condition of paying 1% on goods imported and 3% on exports. Armagaon manufactures a variety of piece goods including suction cotton, chintz, painted pieces of stuff (printed fabrics), and other curious cloth.

Calico-cloth of this area was in high demand.

The Dutch exported salt to Sumatra from this port.

The Dutch had a permanent representative at Quli Qutub Shah Capital. The Dutch Director of Coastal factories had agreed with the Golconda Sultan that the Dutch would pay 300 Pagodas annually, covering all necessary expenses, and to trade freely.

English first settled here in 1626 and abandoned it in1640, favouring Fort St. George.

In 1649, as a further favour, Mir Jumla, Golconda Army General, granted the Dutch trading rights at Allamparwa, north of Pondicherry, a place that was expected to attract cloth manufacturers from Gingee.

The Dutch worked intensely to have the English thrown out of Armagaon. In the first decades of the 17th century, the English were relatively powerless. So they did not enter the power game.

Armagaon was disadvantageous, and unprotected, and the country was in turmoil.

The Dutch needed a factory to store and market their spices for Indian goods, particularly cotton cloth-plain and painted, to sell in the European markets. It was neither convenient for manufacturing nor dying.

It proved Armagaon was not suitable for the continuance of trade.

CHAPTER 14

Sao Tome[33] (St.Thome)/Mylapur (Meliapour)

It is three miles south of Fort St. George. It is one- of the numerous places on the Coromandel Coast. The Portuguese raised it from- near ruin to rich and sumptuous.

In 1661, the Dutch proposed to take it from the Portuguese. But the Golconda Sultan (King) intervened and brought it under his control.

The French wanted to possess St. Thome. They left Ceylon on 09-07-1672 and anchored at St. Thome on 20-07-1672.

On 25-07-1672, they defeated the Golconda army and captured it.

The Dutch army marched on 11-09-1673 to St.Thome, under Rijklot Vangoens from Pulicat, to capture it, from the French.

The French surrendered St. Thome to the Dutch on 23-09- 1674.

The Dutch destroyed the fort and town in October 1675, along with thousands of natives. They

---

[33] *Chennai, Tamil Nadu, India, Zip Code : 600 016*

demolished it, under the orders of the Golconda Sultan.

It was not reconstructed.

In 1749, it was a Portuguese settlement, with new inhabitants.

The English company occupied it, despite Portuguese intrigues.

Sadras[34] (1654-1757) (1785-1795)

Figure 6: Dutch Fort in Sadras

Sadras/Chathurangaapattinam is 64 kilometers from Fort St. George (Madras/Chennai) and 10 kilometers from the tourist place Mahabalipuram. The town was surrounded by weavers' villages and fine muslin cloth weaving centres. It has been under Dutch control, for more than a century. Before the Dutch, it was a centre for muslin cloth, pearls, and edible oil. In 1612, the Dutch established their trading centre at Sadras (Chathurangaapattinam), but in 1648, they started exporting Muslin cloth. With the growing demand for their trade at Sadras (Chathurangaapattinam) in 1654, they built a factory.

---

[34] *Kanchipuram district, Tamil Nadu, India, Zip Code: 603 107*

The English East India Company captured Fort Sadras (Chathurangaahpattinam) in 1749.

The French occupied it in 1758, but the Dutch regained it in 1759.

In 17-02-1782, the first confrontation between the Dutch and English occurred at Sadras (Chathurangapattinam), known as the Battle of Sadras.
They returned the fort to the Dutch in 1784 under the Treaty of Paris, 1784.

In 1796, the English East India Company raided the Factory and destroyed it. They continuously bombarded the fort, from the sea and captured it.

In 1818, the Dutch gained the fort, through a treaty, and rebuilt it.

Finally, on 1st March 1825, the English East India Company took over the factory and the Dutch rule, in India ended.

Sadras (Chathurangaapattinam) was well known for the brick-making industry. The Dutch transported these bricks from Sadras (Chathurangaahpattinam) to Ceylon (now, Srilanka), Batavia (now, Jakarta, Indonesia), and all of their trade centres on the Coromandel Coast. These bricks were used, - to build the forts there, while others were being shipped to European countries.

From the materials and structure found in the Forts, the culture and lifestyle of the Dutch can be evaluated. They led a good life of drinking, smoking, and dancing at Sadras (Chathurangapattinam) Fort. They used little local wares. All wares were from their native countries or other countries. There were two warehouses. The roof was horizontally and vertically punched with holes because of bombardment. They lay on the floor with buried brick tiles. They used an advanced underground drainage system in the fort. The drains from different directions collect at a chamber at the northeast corner-under the warehouse to drain into the sea.

They lay their rooms with rectangular, square, and hexagonal bricks, at the fort, and dressed them with granite slabs. The Dutch fort has a vast compound, including structures to mount elephants, for the army.

The Dutch had a weakness for liquor, tobacco and local games. They used Delft blue earthenware, and Gouda smoking (clay) pipes (Gouda is a province of South Holland).

There are two tombstones in Sadras (Chathurangapattinam).

CHAPTER 16

Pondicherry

Puducherry[35] was the traditional name, corrupted to Pondicherry. And Puducherry was derived from the Tamil word Putucceri: - Pudu means a new and cceri village or town. The name, therefore translates to new town.

Portuguese set up the first factory in Pondicherry, in the 16th century. The French set their foot in Pondicherry- when the Bijapur Sultan of Gingee started trade relations in 1670.

After the French colonization of India, it is called the French Riviera of the- east.

The Dutch seized the Pondicherry-fortress on 3rd September, 1693. French commander, Francois Martin, surrendered the fort. Then the Dutch strengthened the defences of the fortress to make it impregnable.

In addition to European luxury goods, the merchant mariners' imported, dry fruits, pearls, amber, silver, and horses from Persia.

Chintz, white cloth, lungees, unbleached cloth, coarse cloth, and handkerchiefs were purchased by the merchants and carried to Pondicherry by bullock carts from Masulipattam[23], Yaanaon[11], and Narsapur[20]- for bleaching and export.

Brick manufacturing was another important small-scale industry in the region.

---

[35] *India, Zip Code: 605 001.*

The Dutch minted coins at Pondicherry-modelled on the local coins, from 1693 to 1698.

The Dutch were the originator of the current urban development of Pondicherry.

The plans of streets or lanes built, during French Commander, Francois Martin's time, were in an irregular pattern, without any shape or symmetry.

In the plans drafted, during the Dutch occupation, in 1694, there were new towns, with regular geometrical layouts, including rectangular blocks of houses, separated by straight streets that intersected at right angles.

It is proof of the hard-working and God-fearing nature of Dutch Calvinists.

During the first half of the 18th century, the French adopted the urban projects of the Dutch.
The Dutch returned Pondicherry to the French, under the Treaty of Ryswick, 1699.

In 1761, the English, under Sir Eyre Coot, gained control of Pondicherry from the French.

CHAPTER 17

Tierepoplier[36] / (Tirupapuliyur) (1608-1625)

It is in Cuddalore town, two hundred kilometres South of Chennai.

It was in Gingee territory, under the control of the Vijayanagar Emperor, at Vellore. Krishnappa Naik[37] was the ruler of the Gingee region.

In 1608, the Dutch established their factory, here, under chief factor Bourgonje.

After establishing the factory at Tierepopelier (Thirupapuliyur), the Dutch faced conflict with the chief minister of the Tierepopelier (Thirupapuliyur). He is known as Great ayah, meaning older man.

The Great ayyah borrowed some labourers from the Dutch, but he did not let them return. As a result, it held up the work in the Dutch factory.

Eventually, the labourers could return to Dutch. But the Great ayyah did not permit the Dutch to construct a fort in Tierepopelier (Thirupapuliyur), citing that Carnatic/ Vijayanagar king might object to it.

In the spring of 1610, the Dutch factors at Tierepopelier (Thirupapuliyur) received instructions

---

from Bantam (Jakarta, Indonesia) to strengthen the defences of the factory and seek a renew of the factory contract.

They renewed the contract on 29-3-1610. The Great ayyah reduced the tax payable by the company to 2%, for both exports and imports. At the same time, it required the company to pay a cost price, on articles ordered by the King, and available in its territory.

It was not as convenient as Pulicat. Even so, the trade steadily improved by 1617.

The Dutch constructed a building for ammunition and merchandise in Tierepopelier (Thirupapuliyur).

In July 1618, there was a civil war among the Naiks of the region. It forced the Dutch to leave Tierepopelier (Thirupapuliyur).

In 1625, the Dutch returned from Tegenapattam[38] (Devenaampattinam) and reopened the factory at Tierepopelier (Thirupapuliyur). They found the factory was burnt and destroyed. They learned it was by the local chief.

From 1629, a new toll came into force, abolishing the earlier toll, fixed in 1612- at 11/2 % for loading and 21/2%- for unloading of cargo.

The great Ayyah undertook, to force all weavers, painters, and dyers to continue their contacts with the Dutch. He also launched to protect the Dutch from their enemies. Thus, he excluded the Portuguese and English from the area.

In 1630, the Dutch, with the new factory, enjoyed a position of complete independence, and extended their trade to other regions with more investments.

1758, they closed the factory and moved to Porto-Novo[39].

Among the Dutch traded merchandise, the indigo of the Tierepopelier (Thirupapuliyur) was the best.

CHAPTER 18

Tegenepattam (Devanaampattinam) (1608-1758)

Tegenapattam[38] (Devenaampattinam), in the early medieval period, was known as Kudalur and was called Kudalnaadu. The Portuguese called it Tegenapattam (Devenaampattinam). But, English and Dutch called it Cuddalore, because it is 3 kilometres north of present old Cuddalore.

The town did not attract English merchants. Moreover, massive floods often swept the city. So, from 1624 to 1680, the English carried their trade, along the coast without a permanent base. It is in the north of Pondicherry and was, under the reign of Gingee Nayaks.

Admiral Verhoeff of East India Company sent two yachts, Arent and Valck under the command of Jacob de Bitter from Ache to the Dutch East India Company on the Coromandel Coast. Unfavourable winds drifted the Yachts. Jacob de Bitter and his staff landed in Tegenepattam (Devenampattinam).

Gingee Naayak received the Dutch and invited them to open a trade centre at Tegenapattam (Devenampattinam) in the Cuddalore New Town.

Commander de Bitter conveyed this invitation to his Admiral Verhoeff.

---

[38] *Cuddalore district, Tamil Nadu, India, 607 001.*

The Admiral graciously received the opportunity and sent a Dutch commission to Gingee for trade negotiations with Naayak- in November 1608

Krishnappa Naayak II, the Ginjee chief, permitted the Dutch to trade and issued them Olla (Farmanah) on 30-11-1608.

Before the Europeans appeared on the Coromandel Coast, there was an old Indian Fort, on the north bank of of Gadilam River. The Nayak permitted the Dutch to build a fort on the dilapidated old Fort.

Krishnappa Nayak fixed a 4% duty on imports and exports. He exempted the Dutch from tax payment, on factory provisions and import of gold.

In 1608, the Dutch began the construction of the fort. The Portuguese, who could not digest the entry of the Dutch, pressured the Gingee overlord at Vellore, Venkatapathi Rayalu-or Venkata I of Vijayanagara Empire, through a letter from Phillip III, the King of Portugal. This prevented the Dutch from constructing the fort.

Emperor Venkatapathi Rayalu forced on Krishnappa Nayak to withdraw the Farmanah, issued to the Dutch.

However, in 1610, the Dutch recovered the fort and commenced their trading activities in Tegenapattam (Devanaampattinam). The port is in Cuddalore new town, and three kilometres north of old Cuddalore.

Steadily, the Dutch realized the factory on the old Fort, was uninhabitable. They vacated it- in 1625.

In 1628, they took permission from the Ginjee Nayak, to occupy old fort in the neighbouring village, at Tierepopelier[36] (Thirupapuliyur). The Dutch factory at Tegenapattam (Devanaampattinam) was taken over by Gingee Nayak.

In 1676 the Marathas raided and occupied the Gingee- kingdom. They called it Cindy, and consequently, the Tegenapattam (Devanaampattinam) came under the Maratha's rule.

The Dutch returned to Tegenapattam (Devanaampattinam) sometimes, before 1678.

In 1678, the Dutch quit Tegenapattam (Devanaampattinam). They shifted to Pulicaat, partly owing to a dispute with Marathas, over shipping matters at Porto Novo and partly due to their disagreement with their superiors, at headquarters in Batavia (Jakarta, Indonesia). The directors reduced the staff salaries and allowances at Tegenapattam (Devenaampattinam).

They moved towards Cuddalore and built a small, fort there.

The Gedilam River was small, but convenient for the import and export of merchandise,

However, the river could receive 200 tons of ships in September and October. The Dutch established a factory at Tegenapattam (Devenaampattinam) in about 1670 and later built a fort 700 yards north of the mouth of the Gadilan River.

The Dutch used Tegenapattam (Devenaampattinam) port for Coastal trade. In 1680, the Dutch returned to Tegenapattam (Devenaampattinam) and got a grant of land and permission from Marathas to erect a factory.

In 1690, the Maratha ruler, Raja Ram, the son of Chattrapathi Sivaji, was seized in Gingee Fort by the Moghul Emperor's army. For 90,000 pagodas, he sold Tegenapattam (Devenaampattinam) and the surrounding towns and villages- within the range of a shot of a piece of the canon, to the highest bidder-the English, who outbid the Dutch and the French.

They fired cannons in different directions, from the compass, and areas within its range, including the town of Cuddalore, passed to the English. The territory is 13 kilometers, along the coast and 7 kilometers of land.

The English got the old fort, near the Gadilam River and named it Fort St. David, after a Welsh Saint David. The English converted it into a military town.
The Dutch were allowed open trade, but were bound to pay customs duty-to the English East India Company.

When the English bought the fort, the Dutch had a Tegenapattam (Devenaampattinam) factory, about one and a half kilometres, to the north, of the Fort. They were staying there with a few factory- workers. They also had a nearby village, ManjaKuppam, under a lease-for three years.

Manjakuppam was the official centre of Cuddalore.

In 1691 the Dutch asserted their right to Manjakuppam and tried to turn the factory into a fort by massing troops from other Dutch possessions.

But, from the writings in the charter- it was granted to the English.

In August 1691, the English took control of the ManjaKuppam. They had the right over it.

The English were justified to be the proprietor of the Tegenapattam (Devenaampattinam) factory, as well.

But the Dutch chief at Tegenampattam factory, threatened to take possession of the factory and hoist the Dutch flag-by force. factory there. During the French seizure of Fort St. David, in 1757, the English destroyed the Dutch Factory. They were compensated by the English, by giving a house in Cuddalore a new town.

In 1758, the Dutch quit their house and business at Tegenapattam (Devanampattinam) and returned to Porto-Novo[39].

CHAPTER 19

Porto-Novo (1608-1825)

Porto-Novo[39] was an important trading port for Arabs and Yemenis. Locally it is called Parangipettai. In Tamil Parangi means Europeans and pettai refer to a place; therefore Parangipettrai denotes a European place.

After being chased away from Ceylon (Sri Lanka) and other settlements by the Dutch, the Portuguese came with the households to this place. The Port, which was a haven for indigenous merchants, flourished into a well-built town. Hence the Portuguese settled here. In 1590, the Portuguese established their factory, here. It is 29 kilometres south of Pondicherry[35].

Porto translates to Port and Novo means new, which is called a new port.

In 1608 the Dutch established their trading post here. It was under the Gingee kingdom. The chief minister or Ayya of Gingee promised the Dutch he would protect them at Porto-Novo. The Dutch, on its side, promised the chief minister, they would supply, at a cost price, the commodities from territories- under its control. Ayya and Nayak also got the right to buy sulphur, from the Dutch, before all other merchants.

The hinterland of Porto-Novo was rich in rice production was also noted for the manufacturing different kinds of goods. The merchants of Porto-Novo carried cotton cloth, handkerchief, brown cloth, long

---

[39] *Cuddalore district, Tamil Nadu, India Zip Code:608 502*

cloth, Dutch sorts and other things to Pondicherry[35], for shipment-to French territories, and loading them into vessels there.

The Dutch exercised their control over Porto-Novo, uninterrupted, till 1625.

In 1640 the ruler of Bijapur conquered the Porto-Novo region. Shahji, his general, destroyed Porto-Novo, and its merchants were ruined.

In the course of time, Porto Novo recovered, but the trade could not recover as it had moved to Cuddalore.

In 1678, Maratha' leader Shivaji's men attacked the Dutch Factory and plundered 10,000 pagodas from the Dutch. At the same time, the Dutch superiors at Batavia (Jakarta, Indonesia) had diminished and cut off the salaries and allowances of the staff, working at Porto Novo. With no more to exist, at Porto Novo, the Dutch had left for Pulicaat[29].

The English also had a factory at Porto-Novo. Now and then, the French and Danish ships anchored at the port. The Dutch maintained a record of the vessels coming to the Port-it contained the commodity loaded, the port of destination, the number of ports it is touching and the ship's country. In 1764, the Dutch reported that twenty vessels arrived in Porto-Novo the highest percentage, that year.

The Dutch carried out their business from Tegenapattam (Devanampattinam)[38]. In 1680, they returned to Porto-Novo, on the invitation of Arcot Nawab, the fauzidar[40] of the Mughal Emperor. Nawaab gave the Dutch, a concession, in the payment of duties. While the average duty rate was 2.5% on exports, the Dutch paid 1% duty.

The bulk of people is Pagans.

The Dutch shifted their business again to Devenampattinam and, after a few years in, 1758, returned to Porto Novo.

In 1778, Nawab of Mysore, Hyder Ali, sacked the Dutch Porto- Novo factory.

In the Fourth Anglo-Dutch War, in 1781, the English captured all Dutch factories along the beach- including Porto Novo, to prevent the Nawab of Mysore, Hyder Ali, from using any port on the beach.

In the Treaty of Paris, the English returned the factory to the Dutch, as part of the peace agreement.

During French Revolution (1785-95), the English retook Porto-Novo from the Dutch to be returned to them in 1818.

Finally, in June 1825, the English took over the Port.

Alexander Hamilton[41] described Porto-Novo, when he visited between 1688 and 1720; he described it as a fertile, healthy, and pleasant land.

---

40 *Faujidhar: Officer in charge of local administration.*
41 *Alexander Hamilton: An interloper came to India, for trading and not an official of East India Company. He travelled extensively on the Indian Coast between 1688 to 1783.*

It produced good cotton cloth of several qualities and denominations, which they exported to Pego Port, Bago (Myanmar), Kedah (Malaysia), Johor (Malaysia), and Aachen (Sumatra). Piece goods from the interior of Andhra, steel from western Karnataka, iron nails from Narsapur (Narsaapuram), tobacco from Krishna-Godavari, and Tirunellvelli-earthenware and salt were exported to markets in south-east Asia.

Rice and textiles were exported to Ceylon, and in return, elephants, areca, pepper, spice, coconut, coir products, Palmyra, and timber were imported.

Horses were regularly imported from southern Asian ports, particularly Malacca, and Kedah.

From the markets of temple town-Chidambaram, Salem, Tindivanam, Chennamanaikpalayam, and Naidupeta, the textiles and clothes were coming to Porto-Novo. They were assembled there and shipped.

There were villages- in the hinterland of Porto Novo, where hundreds of painting and weaving professionals were available for hire.

Indigo (required for dyeing the cloth) was manufactured and exported from the region.
Slaves were exported to Ceylon (Sri Lanka), and European countries.

Marakkyars, Tamil Muslims and indigenous merchants were dominant traders at Porto Novo. Marakkayars were the descendants of Arab and Yemen merchants, who married local Tamil women and settled, on the Coromandel Coast. They were the only ship-owning merchants of Porto Novo.

Under Marakkaayars-Port-Novo was the best shipbuilding and repairing yard on the Coromandel Coast. A close friendship existed between the French and the Marakkayar merchants of Pondicherry. Every year one overseas sailing, a French ship was loaded at Porto-Novo.

CHAPTER 20

Tirumalairayanpattinam

On 07-04-609, the Dutch factor at Tegnapattam (Devanapattinam) Bourgonje got a cowle, on Tirumalairayanpattinam[42], and its surrounding areas, from the Thanjavur King, Vijaya Raaghav Naayaka, for a sum of 2,800 pagodas. It was taken for Port at Tirumalairayanpattinam

Cotton fabrics, tablecloths, towels, silk clothes, and handkerchiefs were important textiles, that the Dutch exported from Tirumalairayanpattinam.

---

[42] *Karaikal district, Pondicherry, India, Zip Code: 609 606*

CHAPTER 21

Nagapattinam (Nakapattinam/Negapattam) (1658-1781)

Figure 7: Dutch Fort, Nagapattinam

In 1658, Dutch defeated Portuguese and seized Nagapattinam[43] from them. In 1554, Portuguese established business centre in Nagapattinam. They brought the famous Velankanni Church into Nagapattinam.

Nagapattinam is derived by conjoining two words. Nagar translates to people, who came from Ceylon (the present Sri Lanka) and pattinam means town.

It was a famous port of Chola kings. The Nagore River allowed navigation of vessels up to 200 tonnes.

There is a Buddha vihar at Nagapattinam. It was built by a Chinese king, during Pallava king, Raja Simha period.

The Thanjavur king, Vijaya Raghavendra Naik, who was the ruler of Nagapattinam, attacked Dutch by sea, to get rid of Europeans.

---

[43] *Nagapatinam district, Tamil Nadu, India, Zip Code: 611 001*

But he was defeated. Subsequently, he gave the Dutch freedom from all port customs and right to mint coins at ½ duties.

He also agreed to transfer ten villages held by the Portuguese to the Dutch.

On 5th January, 1662 the transfer affected the following towns:
1. Puthur: Tamil Nadu state, India Zip Code: 609 108
2. Muttam: Tamil Nadu state, India Zip Code: 611 002
3. Poruvacherry: Tamil Nadu state, India Zip Code: 611 108
4. Anthanapettai: Tamil Nadu state, India Zip Code: 611 106
5. Karureppankadu: Tamil Nadu state, India Zip Code: 611 xxx
6. Azhingi Mangalam: Tamil Nadu state, India Zip Code: 611 xxx
7. Sangamangalam: Tamil Nadu state, India Zip Code: 611 108
8. Thiruthinamangalam: Tamil Nadu State, India Zip Code: 611 xxx
9. Manjakollai: Tamil Nadu State, India, Zip Code: 611 106;
10. Nariyankudi: Tamil Nadu State, India, Zip Code: 611 xxx.

In the villages, the Dutch built ten churches and a hospital.

In 1674, Venkoji, who was known as Ekoji, Maratha army chief of Bijapur, defeated Thanjavur ruler, Alagiri. In 1676, he founded the Maratha rule in Thanjavur.

On 30th December 1676, as per the agreement between the Dutch and Thanjavur first Maratha ruler, Sri Ekoji, Naagapattnam were under Dutch Ceylon (Sri Lanka) administration.

When the Portuguese sacked the Dutch from their capital Paliacatta (Pulicaat), the Dutch built a fort, called Fort Vijf Sinnen at Nagapattinam. It was heavily armed. Artillery was shipped from Pulicat to Nagapattinam. It was their capital, from 1690 to 1784. Its head, the Governor activities were to spy on English, in addition to supervising Dutch ports on the Coromandel Coast.

In 1773, the Maratha ruler of Thanjavur took an advance from the Dutch. In June 1778, he compensated it to Dutch, by granting Nagapattinam Port, Nagore shrine along with 277 villages.

In 1780, the Fort Vijf Sinnen was damaged due to heavy floods. The Dutch repaired it, from the rubble. New developments in Europe allowed Britain to take Dutch territories wherever they could. It declared war on the Dutch Republic, citing its participation in the war supplies to the rebels of the American colonists. Reynier Van Vlissen, the Dutch Governor at Nagapattinam, was not aware of the developments in Europe, until June 1781, when Willen Falk, Governor of Ceylon (Trincomalee), brought the news, to his notice.

Soon, Van Vlissingen invited Haider Ali, Nawab of Mysore, for negotiations, on an alliance.

Haider Ali was an ally of the French and he did not trust the English. Earlier in 1781, he raided Dutch outposts, at Pulicat, Sadras and villages, including Nagore near Nagapattinam. He noted that the expected help was not coming from France. So, he formed a defence treaty, with the Dutch- to widen his prestige.

He assured the Dutch on 04-09-1781 to protect Nagapattinam, provided the Dutch garrison helped him, whenever he asked for its help. He ceded Nagore, to the Dutch.

On 22-6-1781, Lord McCartney was sent to Madras, as governor of the English East India Company, with instructions to seize all Dutch settlements on the Coromandel Coast, to prevent Haider Ali, from possessing any ports or using them.

British General Sir Eyre Coote arrived from Calcutta (Bengal) to fight Haider Ali.

On 21-10-1781, the Dutch outpost, Nagore, and on 30-10- 1781, Nagapattinam Fort lost to the English

On 12-11-1781 the war ended, with the capture of Nagapattinam Fort, defeating the strong garrison of Dutch governor and Hyder Ali.

A British force of 4,443 men, under the command of General Hector Munro, with the help of Admiral Hughes from the navy, defeated the Dutch. During the war, most of the Haider Ali cavalry fled and Haider Ali returned to Thanjavur town. Thus, Nagapattinam fell into the hands of the English in 1781.

The English returned all Dutch possessions in India, except Nagapattinam.

Nagapattinam, the capital of Dutch from 1690 to 1781 was a production area and market for odoriferous wood and the substance of spices, pepper and rice and coconut fibre.

It competed, in the sale of textiles, with Pulicat. It exported cotton pieces to Banda, Ambon, Serani and other parts of the East Indies.

There is a stone tablet near a temple, stating that in 1777, the pagoda was built by Dutch governor Reynier Vanvlissinger.

In 1674, they minted pagoda coins at Nagapattinam with 'N' engraved in the Tamil language. The coins were meant for circulation in Ceylon (new name Sri Lanka).

CHAPTER 22

Thoothukudi /Tuticorin (1658)

One of the valuable commodities that India gave to the world market is the pearl. Tuticorin[44] was a centre for pearl-fishery, referred to as Muthunagaram or the city of pearls. Tuticorin is the corrupted name of Thoothukudi. Thoothu means dig in Tamil language and kudi is known as a drink. That is, tap drinking water, by digging small ponds.

Thoothukudi is a Port city. It was a large, prosperous city. In 1532, Portuguese arrived to Tuticorin. They were the first arrived Europeans.

In the 18th century, Tuticorin was the emporium of the cotton trade. The Dutch had traded from their headquarters in Colombo, with Tuticorin, due to its proximity. The Dutch Governor secured the monopoly of the pearl and conch fisheries off the coast of Tirunelveli. It has an excellent harbour, where the Dutch anchored their large vessels in the rainy season. It belonged to Madurai Nayak, who was the lord of Tuticorin. In 1632, the Dutch tried to capture the Tuticorin Fort, but failed.

In 1649, the Dutch made the second attempt to capture the same fort. They were not successful. They burnt the Tuticorin- with the help of the ruler of Kandy (Ceylon, now Sri Lanka)

On 11 February 1658, the Dutch, came in thirty ships, with 3,000 men of different descendants like Muslims, Indonesians, the Dutch, the Sinhalese and the

---

[44] Tuticorin district, Tamil Nadu, India, Zip Code: 628 001

Maravas, in two squadrons, and attacked the Tuticorin harbour. For seven days the Portuguese defended the harbour. On 23rd July 1658, fearing bombardment from the Dutch fleet, under Jan Vander, Portuguese surrendered the Tuticorin Fort, to the Dutch and left.

The Dutch were Protestants and the Portuguese were Catholics. The Dutch after came to power in Tuticorin, drove out the Portuguese priests.

The first protestant influence was felt, in the area with the arrival of the Dutch.

(source: Internet)

Figure 8: Tuticorin: Church built by the Dutch in 1750 AD

In 1750, Dutch built a church, in Tuticorin on the beach road, near our lady of snow Basilica. It is the oldest protestant church. The Dutch East India Company symbol VOC and the year of construction engrave is seen, on the front wall of the church.

The Dutch exported textiles from Tuticorin. They also exported commodities, like Salt Petre, cotton yarn,

90

indigo, senna leaves, diamonds, salt, rice and Palmyra stalks. They were also sending slaves to the East Indies.

Until, the Dutch arrived to Tuticorin, the Portuguese officials were paying a low price to the textile manufacturers, its merchants and rice cultivators. But during the Dutch rule in Tuticorin- in the 17th century, the producers and merchants, received reasonable prices, from Portuguese Therefore, the arrival of the Dutch forced the Portuguese to consider the legitimate demands of the oppressed society.

Pearls fishing in Dutch-controlled Tuticorin Coast:

In the early 1700 AD, for fishing of pearls, on the Tuticorin coast, the Dutch sent out ten or twelve boats in different directions on the sea, to find out the potential pearl fishing locations.

The divers of each ship, jump into the sea, collect oysters from sea-bed, float to the surface and pour them in heaps, on the shore. On the coast, an appraiser evaluates the heaps, from a practical point of view. After expenses, the profit-producing heaps go for selection.

After the source of such heaps with their locations was identified, the fishing was considered at such places. They announced the fishing dates to the public.

On the appointed date, people assemble- in crowds- at the coast, amid drum beating and muskets firing. The excitement of the group was unsurpassable until the Dutch Commissioner arrived from Colombo. He comes with pomp- for the inauguration of the fishing. He orders for opening of the fishery, with a salute of cannons. On the appointed day of fishing, boats with divers go to the sea, preceded by two Dutch vessels— the Dutch vessels standout in the sea at fishing borders. The divers on each ship jump into the sea.

The divers provided with sacks for collection of oysters. A massive stone was tied to each diver's foot to sink rapidly. Rope tied around the waist of the diver while the other end through a pulley passes to the boat staff. When caught up with breathing, the divers pull a string, offered to them signalling the boat staff, to pull them up. When the first batch divers flushed out, the second batch of divers jumps into the sea.

When the second batch divers return, the first batch divers will be ready, taking their time, for jumping into the sea. It goes on until afternoon when the divers get weary. A keen diver can dive up to 7 to 8 times. No kits stocked, aiding the breathing, beneath the sea.

Afternoon boats carrying the cargo return to the shore and unload them inside the park, in an open area. They dry their catch for 2 to 3 days, and at the end of the 3rd day, the pearls, from shells would be washed and placed in metal receptacles. After their classification and valuation, the Dutch take the most elegant jewels. But, the first day pearls go to King. It was reserved for him.

Merchants advance money for pearl catch. If there was no catch, they were the loser for the investment.

CHAPTER 23

Thiruchendur[45]

Tirumala Naik was the ruler of Tuticorin.

The Dutch were in war, with Portuguese from 1646 to 1648, at Tuticorin.

In the war, Tuticorin ruler supported the Portuguese.

On March 1, 1649 the Dutch, in retaliation to Tirumala Naik support to Portuguese, seized the Thiruchendur Murugan temple in Tuticorin.

From 6th March 1649, the locals tried to free the temple.

Tirumala Naik also instructed the Dutch to release the temple.

On 25th March 1649, the Dutch vacated the temple, but they fled, with the chief deity of the temple. They demanded a ransom of one lakh Reals for God, from Dutch Ceylon (Sri Lanka)

In February 1651, they brought the idol to Kaaveripatnam, to sell it for 25,000 to 30,000 Reals. But they did not find buyers. They took the God, back to Dutch Ceylon.

At last, the locals recovered the idol and reinstated in the temple.

---

[45] *Tuticorin district, Tamil Nadu, India, Zip Code: 628 215*

CHAPTER 25

Travancore[46]
(Thiruvanthapuram or
Trivendrum)

Travancore king Marthanda Varma had friendly relations with English East India Company. The Dutch felt their friendship a threat to their business, because they were monopoly in pepper and cinnamon trade in Kerala.

In 1672, the Dutch defeated king Zamorin and reached to peak, in pepper and cinnamon trade.

They signed with Odanaadu king and bought all the pepper raised in the kingdom to ship them to Netherlands.

Travancore king Marthanda Varma, attacked on Odanaadu kingdom, and killed the king.

The governor of Dutch East India Company at Ceylon met Marthanda Varma, but the negotiations failed.

A war broke out on land and sea between the Dutch East India Company and Marthanda Varma in 1/1740. On 10-8-1741, the Dutch ships attacked the Travancore kingdom from Kanyakumari (Cape Comorin) to assault and capture Padmanabhapuram (now, Thiruvananthapuram or Trivandrum).

---

46 *Kerala State, India, Zip Code: 695 001*

Travancore soldiers repelled the attack and hit on Dutch anchored ships. They fought and crushed the Dutch East India Company. They captured Dutch navy commander Captain de Lannoy.

The Travancore King called for the navy chief, captain de Lannoy, and asked him to serve in the Travancore kingdom to develop the Travancore army. The naval commander agreed and worked in the Travancore kingdom. They called it the Battle of Colachel (Kolchak), 1741.

Marthanda Varma died in 1758. His nephew Rama Verma succeeded him.

Captain de Lannoy served under Marthanda Varma and Rama Verma for 36 years. He employed his son Johannes Delannoy as commander of a battalion that received wounds in a skirmish and died in 1765.

Trincomalee (ceylon, now Sri Lanka)

Figure 9: Trincomalee (In the 17th century)

It is a natural deep-water harbour in the Indian Ocean. The Portuguese constructed the Fort in 1623. They called it Fort Trincomalee.

The King of Kandy (Sri Lanka) Sri Rajadhi Raja Singhe, wanted to drive off the Portuguese from Ceylon. So, he invited the Dutch to Ceylon (Sri Lanka)

The Dutch captured the port of Galle, in 1640 from the Portuguese and in 1656 they took Colombo with the help of King Raja Singhe II of Kandy.

After the expulsion of the Portuguese from the area, the Dutch gained control over the coastal region. Consequently, the Dutch acquired monopoly over the spice, cinnamon.

In 1665, the Dutch enlarged the fort and changed its name to Pagoda Hill. The British Prime Minister, Winston Pitt (1766-68), urged the Governor-General of English East India Company, Lord Cornwallis, to seize Trincomalee from the Dutch, so that the French couldn't use it as a base.

The English East India Company boats under Admiral Hughes disembarked at Trincomalee Harbour on January 4 and 5 and took over the fort. The English christened the fort Fort Frederick.

Osterberg Fort: Osterberg Fort means Eastern Fort. King Raja Singhe built this Fort. The English East India Company attacked the Fort on January 11, 1783, and captured it.

Winston Pitt, the British Prime Minister, commented on Osterberg Fort as the finest and most helpful bay of India.

The VOC trade with Europe was 30% and it sent the goods, until 1626, straight to Netherlands. However, after 1626 it despatched goods to Europe, through Batavia (Jakarta, Indonesia)

In conclusion, the VOC earned high profits. It had 150 merchant ships, 40 warships. Further, it had a private army of 50,000 soldiers and it maintained around 50,000 employees.

It was paying a 40% dividend to shareholders, on the original investment. And it was the world's wealthiest private company in the world.

By 1799, the VOC financial performance was reduced. It could not run commercially, meeting with its enormous overhead costs. On the other hand, it could no longer compete with the English, who grew powerful.

Further, the consequences after, IV Anglo-Dutch war and the French invasion on its Republic had disastrous effect on its functioning. It could no longer continue with its business. So, on 31 December, 1799, VOC was dissolved.

By 1820, in India, the Dutch having business rivalry with the English withdraw to Batavia (Jakarta, Indonesia).

The Dutch territories became Dutch Government colonies.